NIGERIA

LETTERS FROM AROUND THE WORLD

Ali Brownlie Bojang

Photographs by Boris Heger

CHERRYTREE BOOKS

LETTERS FROM AROUND THE WORLD

Titles in this series

AUSTRALIA · BANGLADESH · BRAZIL · CANADA · CHINA COSTA RICA · EGYPT · FRANCE · GERMANY · GREECE INDIA · INDONESIA · ITALY · JAMAICA · JAPAN · KENYA MEXICO · NIGERIA · PAKISTAN · RUSSIA · SAUDI ARABIA SOUTH AFRICA · SPAIN · SWEDEN · THE USA

A Cherrytree Book

Conceived and produced by

Nutshell MEDIA

www.nutshellmedialtd.co.uk

First published in 2007 by
Evans Brothers Ltd
2A Portman Mansions
Chiltern Street
London W1U 6NR

VISIT OUR WEBSITE www.evansbooks.co.uk

© Copyright Evans Brothers 2007

Editor: Polly Goodman
Designer: Tim Mayer
Map artwork: Encompass Graphics Ltd
All other artwork: Tim Mayer
All photographs were taken by Boris Heger.

Acknowledgements
The photographer would like to thank Bose and her family, the staff and pupils of her school in Piwoyi, Nigeria, Mr and Mrs Olusola Oladele, and Laurent Meierhans for all their help with this book. The author would like to thank Ronnie Williams for her help with details about Nigerian life and the Yoruba language.

British Library Cataloguing in Publication Data
Brownlie Bojang, Ali, 1949-
  Letters from Nigeria. – (Letters from around the world)
  1. Nigeria – Social life and customs – Juvenile literature
  I. Title
  966.9'054

ISBN-13: 9781842343807

Cover: Bose (centre) with her friends Richard and Bimi.
Title page: At dinner time, the family get together and catch up with everyone's news.
This page: Animals are herded across the Niger river where it meets the Benue river.
Contents page: Bose sets off for school wearing her blue and white school uniform.
Glossary page: Bose and her friend Iyabo return from the well carrying buckets full of water.
Further Information page: Children at Bose's school enjoy a break from their lessons in the school playground.
Index: A woman cooks and sells grilled maize by the side of the road.

Contents

My Country

Monday, 1 April

PO Box 784
Abuja
Nigeria

Dear Billie,

Ekaabo! (You say 'Ek-ah-boe'. This means 'welcome' in Yoruba, my language.)

My name is Bose Obode and I'm 10 years old. I live in a village called Piwoyi, in Nigeria. I have a brother, Godwin, who is 3 and a sister, Happy, who is 1 year old.

I'd really like to hear about your family and where you live. Write back soon!

O da bo! (Bye!)

From

Bose →

Here's my family. I'm at the front, with Godwin and Dad behind me. Happy and Mum are on the right.

4

Nigeria is a large country in West Africa. The population is bigger than any other country in Africa. People have lived there for thousands of years, but the country known as Nigeria today was only formed in 1960.

Nigeria's place in the world.

Nigeria was named after the River Niger, its longest river. Where the Niger meets the sea there is a large delta, called the Niger Delta.

5

The roads in Piwoyi get very muddy in the rainy season. There are lots of market stalls along the main street selling fruit, vegetables and basic goods such as soap and spoons.

Piwoyi is a large village near Abuja, the capital of Nigeria. Both Piwoyi and Abuja were only built in the last forty years. Abuja used to be just a small village. Now it is a big, busy city.

Many people who live in Piwoyi work in Abuja. People have moved to the village from other parts of Nigeria in the hope of getting a job in the capital.

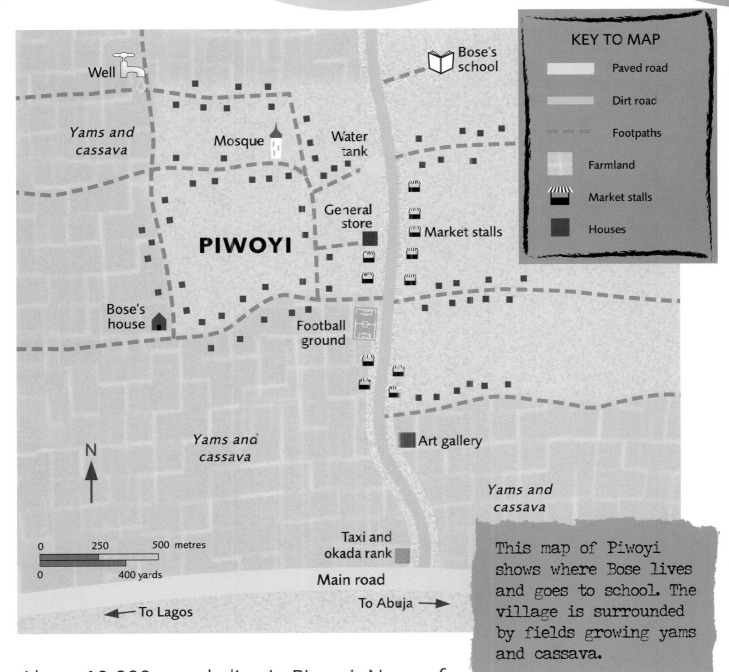

Well

Bose's school

Yams and cassava

Mosque

Water tank

General store

PIWOYI

Market stalls

Bose's house

Football ground

Yams and cassava

Art gallery

Yams and cassava

N

0   250   500 metres

0   400 yards

Taxi and okada rank

Main road

To Lagos   To Abuja →

This map of Piwoyi shows where Bose lives and goes to school. The village is surrounded by fields growing yams and cassava.

About 10,000 people live in Piwoyi. None of the houses has a tap. People have to buy their drinking water in bottles or buckets from a truck that travels around the village. For washing, they collect water from wells or from the river nearby. There is no rubbish collection service, so people take their waste to a dump outside the village. Sometimes they set fire to it.

7

Landscape and Weather

Nigeria has a tropical climate, which means that it is hot all year round. For some months of the year it rains a lot. This is called the rainy season. Then in the dry season it does not rain at all for several months.

This family is planting seeds and preparing the land for the rainy season.

There is much more rain in the south of Nigeria than in the north of the country. In the south, there are tropical rainforests and mangrove forests. In the north, there are dry plains and deserts. In the centre of Nigeria, around Piwoyi, there are hills, forests and good farmland.

In the dry season, farmland has to be watered often. These girls are getting water from a well to put on the crops.

Piwoyi's Climate

January
Temperature
26°C

0mm
Rainfall

July
Temperature
26°C

650mm
Rainfall

At Home

Bose's house has one bedroom, where her parents sleep, a living room, where the children sleep, and a storage room. The walls are made from bricks and it has a corrugated iron roof. The roof makes a rattling noise when the heavy rains come. There is an insect screen on the door that keeps the flies out.

Bose's family always leaves their shoes outside to help keep the house clean. The raised path keeps the mud out in the rainy season.

When the electricity is working, Bose, Happy and Godwin enjoy watching TV and listening to music on the stereo.

Although the houses in Piwoyi have electricity, there are frequent power cuts. So for lighting, Bose's family often has to use kerosene lamps and candles. Some people use car batteries to power their TV sets.

Bose, Godwin and Happy sleep on a mattress on the living room floor. It is put down there every evening.

Bose helps her mother do the laundry outside their house. The clothes dry quickly in the hot sun.

Bose gets up at 6 a.m. every morning to help get breakfast ready and to go to the well. She fetches the water, sweeps the floors and helps keep the house clean and tidy. Bose also helps her mother look after Godwin and Happy. Older girls in Nigeria always look after the younger children.

Bose sells kerosene to the neighbours to make a bit more money for the family. The kerosene is used in lamps.

Wednesday, 6 May

PO Box 784
Abuja
Nigeria

Ekaro (good morning)!

Thanks for your letter. We had to collect it from the post office in Abuja, because there's no postal service in our village. You asked what jobs I have to do at home. The most important one is to collect water from the well, which is a kilometre away from our house. It takes me about an hour to walk to the well and back. I have to go twice a day, once before school and again when I get back. I collect the water in a bucket and carry it on my head.

Why don't you try and do this with an empty bucket? It's not as easy as it looks!

From

Bose

Look – no hands! See how I balance the water! We use the water for washing, cooking and cleaning.

Food and Mealtimes

Bose's mother grows vegetables, such as cassavas and yams, on a small piece of land the family owns. They buy the rest of their food from the general store and market stalls in the village.

Bose gives Godwin and Happy their breakfast. They usually have plain bread and tea.

Dinner is the main meal of the day. Here the family is eating fried beignets (a bit like doughnuts) with custard for pudding.

Bose loves going to the market to do the shopping. She often meets her friends there. She buys fish, meat, vegetables, palm oil, rice and spices. Many different fruits and vegetables grow in Nigeria, such as oranges, bananas, melons, mangos and peppers, yams, cassava, okra and onions.

The general store sells nearly everything the family needs. For anything else, they have to go to Abuja.

Bose's mum cooks outside on a charcoal stove. Charcoal is made from wood. It burns more slowly than wood, so it is good for cooking.

In the evening, Bose's family likes to eat *fu fu*, which is made from pounded cassava, with *obe efo*, a vegetable stew. Sometimes they eat *fu fu* with chicken, goat or beef stew. On special occasions they have *jollof rice*. When Bose's mum cooks, she always makes a lot in case they have visitors.

As she pounds yam with a big mortar and pestle, a woman chats with a neighbour and catches up on the latest news.

Friday, 3 June

PO Box 784
Abuja
Nigeria

Hi Billie,

You asked me for a typical Nigerian recipe. My favourite meal is *jollof rice*. This is how to make it:

You will need: 1 cup of white rice, 4 tomatoes, 1/2 red chilli (if you like spicy food), 1 onion, 1 stock cube.

1. Cut the onion and tomatoes into very small pieces.
2. Ask an adult to chop the chilli into very small pieces. (They will need to wash their hands immediately afterwards because chillies can burn delicate skin.)
3. Cook the rice in about 2 cups of water.
4. Add the stock cube.
5. Add the chopped onions, tomatoes and chilli.
6. Cook for about 15 minutes until the rice is soft.

I hope you like it!

From

Bose

Here's a plate of *jollof rice* that I cooked – delicious!

School Day

Bose's school is 10 minutes' walk away from her home. After doing some chores, Bose walks there with Godwin. Most children in Nigeria walk to school, even if it is a long way away.

Bose likes school. She learns English, science, geography, history and art. Sometimes the classes take place outside, under a tree for shade.

Children run through the school gates, ready for assembly at 8.30 a.m.

In the morning assembly there is always singing, dancing and drumming.

Everyone in Bose's class concentrates hard in lessons. About 7 million children in Nigeria are not able to go to school because their parents cannot afford it.

Bose is lucky. Her parents have enough money to send her to school, which is the only one in the village. Some children in the village don't go to school at all because it costs too much.

The boys at Bose's school enjoy a game of basketball, which is very popular in Nigeria. Some Nigerians have moved to the USA to become professional basketball players.

Bose wears a school uniform that must be ironed every day. Her mother uses a charcoal iron if the electricity is not working. Her hair has to be neat and braided. Boys' hair has to be cut short.

The children who can afford it have lunch at school. They usually have a bowl of plain rice with a chilli sauce.

Tuesday, 7 July

PO Box 784
Abuja
Nigeria

Dear Billie,

Thanks for your last letter. I'm glad you liked the *jollof rice*.

Let me tell you about my school. I started there when I was 4 years old. I work very hard and I'm nearly top of my class. My favourite subject is art, but I also like geography, especially looking at maps of different places in the world. At school we speak English, but at home we speak Yoruba. English is the official language of Nigeria because, in the past, it was ruled by Britain. Do you speak any other languages?

Write back soon.

From

Bose

Look how hard I'm concentrating on drawing this plant in my art class!

Off to Work

Bose's mother has built her own hairdressing salon next to the house. Bose's father is a salesman. He travels all over Nigeria buying and selling lots of different things. Other people in the village run market stalls, drive motorcycle taxis known as *okadas*, or they are farmers.

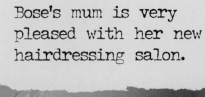

Bose's mum is very pleased with her new hairdressing salon.

A street trader sells biscuits as an *okada* (motorcycle taxi) drives by.

Most people in Nigeria are farmers. Around Bose's village, the farmers grow yams, corn, sweet potatoes, cassavas and other vegetables. But many people are moving to the towns, where they do different jobs like working in shops, factories and offices. Some people work in the oil industry.

This woman is turning corn into flour using a milling machine.

Free Time

Bose's family, like most people in the village, has little spare time. They are usually busy working. But when they do have time off, they go to the river for a picnic and a swim, or visit relatives. Bose loves watching Nigerian films at the village video club.

Many people don't have their own video player. They pay to watch films in the video club instead.

A friend of Bose's family has a board game. They take turns at throwing the dice and moving their counters on the board.

Saturday, 31 July

PO Box 784
Abuja
Nigeria

Hi Billie,

Thanks for your letter. You asked about the toys I have and the games I play. I don't have any toys. I meet my friends in a big open space in the middle of the village, called the *ama*. We play clapping or tickling games where we make each other laugh. The boys like trying to hit a stone by throwing bottle tops at it. We have lots of games, but none of them needs anything except maybe a few stones and bottle tops.

From

Bose

Here I am with my friend Deborah playing a clapping game. We move our hands faster and faster, until we go wrong and collapse in giggles!

Religion and Special Days

Bose and her family are Christians. About half of all Nigerians are Christians. The other half are Muslims. Every Sunday, the family travels to Abuja to go to church. There are about 4,000 people in the congregation. The service is broadcast outside for those who cannot fit into the church.

Bose and her family wear their best clothes to go to church.

Most people who live in northern Nigeria are Muslims. These Muslims are praying in a mosque.

One of the main celebrations for Muslims in Nigeria is Eid ul-Fitr, which takes place at the end of the month of Ramadan. Christians celebrate Christmas and Easter. Both Christians and Muslims celebrate naming ceremonies, when families and friends get together to celebrate the naming of a new baby.

Food is an important part of a naming ceremony. All the women help to prepare the feast of fried fish and *jollof rice*.

Fact File

Capital city: The capital of Nigeria is Abuja. It became the capital in 1976. In this photo you can see the central mosque in the background.

Other major cities: Lagos is the largest city in Nigeria. It used to be the capital, before Abuja. Kano is the main city in the north.

Size: 923,769km^2.

Population: 131,859,731. Nigeria has the largest population in Africa. There are over 250 different ethnic groups. The main ones are the Yoruba, the Hausa, the Ibo and the Fulani.

Flag: The colours of the Nigerian flag have special meanings. The green stands for farming and the richness of the land. White stands for peace.

Longest river: The Niger river is 4,200km long. It is the longest river in Nigeria and the whole of West Africa. This photo shows the point where the Niger meets the Benue river. You can see the camps of animal herders in the centre.

Currency: The naira (N). There are 100 kobo in 1 naira.

Languages: There are over 500 languages in Nigeria. English is the official language, but Yoruba, Hausa and Ibo are all national languages.

Highest mountain: Chappal Waddi (2,419m).

Wildlife: Nigeria used to have lots of wild animals, such as lions and elephants, but forest clearance and building work has driven many away. However, you can still see gorillas, chimpanzees, monkeys, parrots and lots of different butterflies.

Main religions: Islam in the north, Christianity in the south. Traditional African religions everywhere.

Main industries: Oil is the most important industry in Nigeria.

History: People have lived in Nigeria for over 2,200 years, but the country called Nigeria today was only formed in 1960, when it became independent from British rule.

Famous people: Fela Kuti (1938–97) was a famous Nigerian musician and human rights activist. Ben Okri (born in 1959) and Chinua Achebe (born in 1930) are famous writers. Pop stars Sade (born in 1959) and Seal (born in 1963) have Nigerian parents.

Stamps: Nigerian stamps show famous people, buildings or wildlife.

Glossary

charcoal A material made from wood that is burned in fires for cooking.

corrugated iron Sheets of iron often used for roofing.

delta Where a river meets the sea and spreads out, forming lots of islands.

desert An area of very dry land that has very little rainfall.

dry season The months of the year when very little rain falls.

fu fu A dish made from pounded cassava, a little like mashed potato.

kerosene A fuel used for lamps.

mangrove forests Forests of trees that grow on muddy coasts, with long roots that reach above the mud.

mortar and pestle A bowl and a heavy, blunt instrument used for grinding food.

mosque A place where Muslims go to pray and hold religious ceremonies.

naming ceremony A ceremony at which a baby is given a name.

palm tree A type of tree that grows in hot climates.

power cuts When electricity is cut off.

rainy season A few months of the year when most of the rain falls.

settlement A collection of houses where people live, such as a village or a town.

tarmac The material used to make a road and produce a smooth surface.

tropical The area between the Tropic of Cancer and the Tropic of Capricorn. Tropical areas have a hot, dry season and a hot, rainy season.

Further Information

Information books:

Ebele's Favourite: A Book of African Games by Ifeoma Onyefulu (Frances Lincoln, 2000)

One Big Family: Sharing Life in an African Village by Ifeoma Onyefulu. (Frances Lincoln, 1999)

A Triangle for Adaora by Ifeoma Onyefulu (Frances Lincoln, 2001)

Here Comes Our Bride!: An African Wedding Story by Ifeoma Onyefulu (Frances Lincoln, 2004)

Welcome to My Country: Nigeria by Esther Kerr (Franklin Watts, 2005)

Fiction:

Anansi the Spider by G McDermot (Holt, 1987) A traditional Yoruba story.

The Coming of Night: A Yoruba Creation Myth from West Africa by James Riordan (Frances Lincoln, 2006)

Why the Sky is Far Away: A Nigerian Folktale by Mary-Joan Gerson (Little Brown, 2005)

Resource pack:

Hands-on Africa: Art Activities for All Ages by Yvonne Y Merrill (Kits Publishing, 2000)

Websites:

Motherland Nigeria
www.motherlandnigeria.com
Click on 'Kidzone' for Nigerian stories and games, plus an introduction to Nigerian languages.

The World Factbook
www.cia.gov/cia/publications/factbook
Facts and figures about Nigeria and other countries.

Index